Part I
THE STORY OF FATIMA

On a cool spring day in 1916, Lucy dos Santos, age 9, and her cousins, Francisco and Jacinta Marto, ages 8 and 6 respectively, took their parents' sheep to pasture in a place not far from their homes in the mountain village of Fatima, Portugal, about 90 miles north of Lisbon. It started to drizzle, and the children sought shelter in a nearby cave. Suddenly across the field, a white globe of light appeared, moving over the open space toward the cave. The three children stared in awe as they saw in the center of the light a beautiful young man in flowing white garments.

The stranger began to speak: *"Fear not. I am the Angel of Peace. Pray with me."* Kneeling on the ground, he bowed low and recited this prayer three times, with the children repeating it after him: *"O my God, I believe, I adore, I hope and I love Thee. I ask pardon for those who do not believe, do not adore, do not hope and do not love Thee."*

In mid-summer, as the children were together, the Angel came again, and said, *"Pray! Pray a great deal. The Hearts of Jesus and Mary have merciful designs on you. Offer prayers and sacrifices continually to the Most High. Make everything you do a sacrifice, and*

1

offer it as an act of reparation for the sins by which God is offended, and as a petition for the conversion of sinners. Bring peace to our country in this way . . . I am the Guardian Angel of Portugal. Accept and bear with submission all the sufferings the Lord will send you."

The Angel came again in the fall of that same year, this time bearing a golden chalice in one hand and a Host above it in the other. The amazed children noticed that drops of blood were falling from the Host into the chalice. Presently the Angel left both suspended in mid-air and prostrated himself on the ground, saying this beautiful prayer: *"Most Holy Trinity—Father, Son, and Holy Spirit—I adore Thee profoundly. I offer Thee the most precious Body, Blood, Soul and Divinity of Jesus Christ, present in all the tabernacles of the world, in reparation for the outrages, sacrileges and indifferences whereby He is offended. And through the infinite merits of His Most Sacred Heart and the Immaculate Heart of Mary, I beg of Thee the conversion of poor sinners."*

Such was the prelude to one of the most remarkable messages ever to be given from Heaven to Earth—the "peace plan" of Our Lady of Fatima.

THE LADY "MORE BRILLIANT THAN THE SUN"

On Sunday, May 13, 1917, slightly more than a year after the Angel's first visit, the children were pasturing their flocks as usual. This time they were in a rather barren hollow, known as the Cova da Iria (Hollow of Irene), which was about a mile from their homes. It was noon of a clear, sunny day, when suddenly a flash of lightning cut the air—then another. Fearing a storm, the children quickly gathered the sheep to get them home. Then their glances fell upon a small holm-oak tree directly in their path. A dazzling light hovered over the topmost branches, when—wonder of wonders—what should they behold but the form of a lovely lady standing atop the tree in the light, her feet hidden in a shimmering cloud. She was like the Angel, only far more beautiful. She wore a long white dress, and the mantle over her head and shoulders reaching to her feet was edged in burnished gold. Her hands were joined before her breast, and from the right hand hung an exquisite rosary of white pearls. As Lucy later described her, *"She was a lady more brilliant than the sun."*

After telling the children not to be frightened, the vision said: *"I come from Heaven. I want you to come here at this same hour on the 13th day of each month until October. Then I will tell you who I am and what I want."* She also told them to say the Rosary every day, and to bear all the sufferings God would send them.

In June the Lady appeared again. There were about 70 people present, though only the children could see the apparition. She told the youngsters that many souls go to Hell because they have no one to pray and make sacrifices for them. She said Francisco and Jacinta would soon leave the world for Heaven. Holding out her heart surrounded by thorns which pierced it from all sides, Our Lady told Lucy: *"God wishes you to remain in the world for some time because He wants to use you to establish in the world the devotion to my Immaculate Heart. I promise salvation to those who embrace it, and their souls will be loved by God as flowers placed by myself to adorn His throne."*

During her appearance in July, Our Lady, in answer to Lucy's plea, promised that in October she would work a great public miracle so that all might believe and know who she was. Again the Mother of God told the children to sacrifice themselves for sinners and to say many times, especially when making a sacrifice, this prayer: *"O my Jesus, I offer this for love of Thee, for the conversion of poor sinners, and in reparation for all the sins committed against the Immaculate Heart of Mary."*

As she spoke these words, Our Lady stretched out her hands, and bright rays came forth which seemed to penetrate into the earth. All at once the ground vanished, and the children found themselves standing on the brink of a sea of fire. As they peered into this dreadful place, the terrified youngsters saw huge numbers of devils and damned souls. The devils resembled hideous black animals, each filling the air with despairing shrieks. The damned souls were in their human bodies and seemed to be brown in color, tumbling about constantly in the flames and screaming with terror. All were on fire within and without their bodies, and neither devils nor damned souls seemed able to control their movements. They were tossing about in the flames like fiery coals in a furnace. There was never an instant's peace or freedom from pain.

Looking with compassion at the pale and trembling little ones, the vision spoke to them: *"You have seen Hell, where the souls of poor sinners go. To save them, God wishes to establish in the world the devotion to my*

Immaculate Heart. If people do what I tell you, many souls will be saved and there will be peace."

THE VISION FORETELLS WORLD WAR II AND COMMUNISM

"The war [First World War, then raging] is going to end. But if people do not stop offending God, another and worse one will begin in the reign of Pius XI. When you shall see a night illuminated by an unknown light [January 25, 1938], know that this is the great sign that God gives you that He is going to punish the world for its many crimes by means of war, hunger, and persecution of the Church and the Holy Father.

"To prevent this, I shall come to ask for the consecration of Russia to my Immaculate Heart and the Communion of Reparation on the five first Saturdays. If my requests are granted, Russia will be converted and there will be peace. If not, she will scatter her errors throughout the world, provoking wars and persecution of the Church. The good will be martyred, the Holy Father will have much to suffer, and various nations will be destroyed . . .

". . . But in the end, my Immaculate Heart will triumph, the Holy Father will consecrate Russia to me, Russia will be converted, and a certain period of peace will be granted to the world." The Lady asked that this message be kept secret until she gave permission to reveal it.

THE CHILDREN ARE JAILED

The apparitions rapidly were creating so much excitement that the atheistic civil authorities became alarmed. At the next scheduled appearance of the Lady, August 13th, though more than 15,000 people were waiting in the Cova, the atheistic mayor of Ourem, under whose jurisdiction Fatima belonged, had the children kidnapped and placed in jail. In spite of his threats to have them burnt alive in boiling oil, the children refused to reveal the secret given to them. Fearing violence from the people, the mayor released Lucy and her cousins the next day. Near the village of Valinhos on August 19th, the Lady appeared to the children again. She told them she was greatly displeased by the action of the mayor. As a result, the miracle promised for October would not be as impressive as originally planned.

More than 30,000 people were present in September, and saw a shower of mysterious white petals fall to within 10 feet of the ground before dissolving into the air. Many also saw the globe of light bearing the Lady come to rest atop the tree, and the branches bend as though someone were standing on them. Later, they saw the cloud depart into the east, from whence it had come.

70,000 GATHER
FOR THE PROMISED MIRACLE

By now, all Portugal was stirred by the events taking place at Fatima, suddenly the most important spot in the land. Particularly were the newspapers interested, especially in the statement that a great miracle was to take place. Many reporters and photographers were on hand to record the events, or to prove that the statements were nothing more than lies.

On the days preceding October 13th, all roads led to Fatima, with people coming from all parts of the land in any form of transportation they could find. Many walked for miles over the rough fields. It rained all the night of the 12th and the morning of the 13th. By noon, more than 70,000 had crowded into the Cova. Standing in mud up to their ankles, they huddled together under umbrellas, seeking protection from the relentless rain as they prayed their rosaries.

Shortly after noon the Lady arrived for her final appearance. She told the children:

"I am the Lady of the Rosary. I have come to warn the faithful to amend their lives and to ask pardon for their sins. They must not offend Our Lord any more, for He is already too grievously offended by the sins of men. People must say the Rosary. Let them continue saying it every day."

THE SUN WHIRLS IN THE SKY

As the Lady was about to leave, she pointed to the sun. Lucy excitedly repeated the gesture, and the people looked into the sky. The rain had ceased, the clouds parted, and the sun shone forth, but not in its usual brilliance. Instead, it appeared like a silver disc, pale as the moon, at which all could gaze without straining their eyes. Suddenly, impelled by some mysterious force, the disc began to whirl in the sky, casting off great shafts of multicolored light. Red, green, blue, yellow, violet—the enormous rays shot across the sky at all angles, lighting up the entire countryside for many miles around, but particularly the upturned faces of those 70,000 spell-bound people. After three minutes the wonder stopped, but was resumed again a second and a third time—three times in all—within about 12 minutes. It seemed that the whole world was on fire, with the sun spinning at a greater speed each time.

Then a gasp of terror rose from the crowd, for the sun seemed to tear itself from the heavens and come crashing down upon the horrified multitude. *"It's the end of the world!"* shrieked one woman. *"Dear God, don't let me die in my sins!"* implored another. *"Holy Virgin, protect us!"* cried a third. All were on their knees in terror, asking pardon for their sins. Just when it seemed that the ball of fire would fall upon and destroy them, the miracle ceased and the sun resumed its normal place in the sky, shining forth as peacefully as ever.

When the people arose from the ground, cries of astonishment were heard on all sides. Their clothes, which had been soaking wet and muddy, now were clean and dry. Many of the sick and crippled had been cured of their afflictions.

THE CHILDREN ENJOY SPECIAL VISIONS

While the miracle of the sun was taking place, the children alone were privileged to witness several remarkable visions in the heavens. As Our Lady had promised, St. Joseph had come with the Holy Family and he had blessed the world. Then, Our Lady appeared as the Mother of Sorrows, accompanied by her Divine

Son, who also blessed the world. Finally, Lucy had seen the Blessed Virgin Mary, dressed in the brown robes of Our Lady of Mount Carmel, crowned as Queen of Heaven and Earth, holding a brown Scapular in her hand, with her infant Son upon her knee. However, in none of these visions had any of the figures spoken to the children.

Truly, it had been a great day for Portugal. The reporters, many of whom had come to scoff, gave long and detailed accounts of what had taken place, while the newspapers published many photographs of the great crowds and of the children. Although these were released to the entire world (copies are on file in the U.S. Congressional Library), few people outside Portugal paid any attention to these events, and newspapers in most other countries ignored the story completely.

Part II
SUBSEQUENT IMPORTANT EVENTS

As the Blessed Mother had promised, Francisco and Jacinta soon joined her in Heaven. The little boy died from the flu in April, 1919 and his sister from pleurisy in February, 1920.

Before she died, little Jacinta revealed some little-known but remarkable statements made by Our Lady of Fatima. Here are some of them:

"More souls go to Hell because of sins of the flesh than for any other reason."

"Certain fashions will be introduced that will offend Our Lord very much."

"Many marriages are not good; they do not please Our Lord and are not of God."

"Priests must be pure, very pure. They should not busy themselves with anything except what concerns the Church and souls. The disobedience of priests to their superiors and to the Holy Father is very displeasing to Our Lord."

"The Blessed Mother can no longer restrain the hand of her Divine Son from striking the world with just punishment for its many crimes."

"If the government of a country leaves the Church in peace and gives liberty to our Holy Religion, it will be blessed by God."

"Tell everybody that God gives graces through the Immaculate Heart of Mary. Tell them to ask graces from her, and that the Heart of Jesus wishes to be venerated together with the Immaculate Heart of Mary. Ask them to plead for peace from the Immaculate Heart of Mary, for the Lord has confided the peace of the world to her."

OUR LADY APPEARS WITH THE CHRIST CHILD TO SISTER LUCIA

In 1921, upon the advice of the Bishop of Leiria-Fatima, Lucy entered a convent boarding school to learn to read and write. Later she became a nun in the order, a Sister of St. Dorothy, whose motherhouse was at Tuy, Spain.

One day, while Lucy (now Sister Lucia) was kneeling in prayer in the convent chapel (December 10, 1925), the Blessed Mother and the Christ Child appeared to her with a new and wonderful message for souls. The first to speak was the Christ Child, who said: *"Have pity on the heart of your Most Holy Mother. It is covered with thorns with which ungrateful men pierce it at every moment, and there is no one to remove them with an act of reparation."*

Holding in her hand a heart encircled with sharp thorns, Our Lady then said to Sister Lucia: *"My child, behold my heart surrounded with the thorns which ungrateful men place therein at every moment by their blasphemies and ingratitude. You at least try to console me. Announce in my name that I promise to assist at the hour of death with all the graces necessary for salvation, all those who, on the first Saturday of five consecutive months, go to Confession and receive Holy Communion, recite the Rosary, and keep me company for a quarter of an hour while meditating on the mysteries of the Rosary, with the intention of making reparation to me."*

SISTER LUCIA'S SECRET

Our Lord appeared to Sister Lucia in 1927, this time giving her permission to reveal the first two parts of the message of Fatima: 1) The vision of Hell, including the promise to take the children to Heaven, the predictions of another war, martyrdom for Christians, the destruction of nations, the persecution of the Church and of the Holy Father, and the spread of Communism. 2) The devotion to the Immaculate Heart of Mary. All this had previously been kept secret.

In 1929, Our Lady came once again. She completed the promise made on July 13th to come and ask for the consecration of Russia to the Immaculate Heart of Mary and the Communion of Reparation on the First Saturdays. *"The moment has come in which God asks the Holy Father, in union with all the bishops of the world, to make the consecration of Russia to my Immaculate Heart, promising to save it by this means. There are so many souls whom the Justice of God condemns for sins committed against me, that I have come to ask reparation: sacrifice yourself for this intention and pray."* If men would fulfill her requests, Russia would be converted and there would be peace.

There is still an unknown part of the message of Fatima that has never been revealed. Prior to 1950, Sister Lucia wrote down this secret and placed it in an envelope which was sealed and given to the Bishop of Fatima to be opened in 1960. [Editor's Note: In 1960 the letter was opened, and its contents were read by Pope John XXIII. At that time, ecclesiastical authorities decided not to reveal it to the general public. No one in authority had ever said the secret would be *revealed* to the world, but only that the letter would be *opened* in 1960.]

On the night of January 25, 1938, Sister Lucia stood at her convent window and saw an ominous red glow that lit the entire sky. This light was seen throughout

Europe and Africa and in part of America and Asia. Scientists tried to explain it as a most unusual display of the Aurora Borealis, or Northern Lights. But Sister Lucia knew that it was the great sign foretold by Our Lady on July 13, 1917, and that the punishment of the world was at hand. Several weeks later, Hitler invaded Austria striking the match that was to set the world aflame. Thus began another and worse war in the reign of Pius XI, as predicted by the Mother of God at Fatima.

ECCLESIASTICAL APPROVAL FOR THE MESSAGE OF FATIMA

The Bishop of Leiria-Fatima, after 13 years of thorough and careful investigation, released in 1930 his pastoral letter stating that the revelations at Fatima were worthy of belief by the faithful. Today, in the place where the Blessed Mother appeared to the children as they pastured their sheep, there is now a magnificent shrine, where millions of people come on pilgrimage each year.

Pope Pius XII, on October 31, 1942, personally consecrated the world to the Immaculate Heart of Mary. Not long after, he instituted throughout the universal Church the Feast of the Immaculate Heart of Mary, which is celebrated everywhere in the world on the Saturday after the Feast of the Sacred Heart of Jesus.

On May 1, 1948, Pope Pius XII issued a special encyclical letter to all the bishops, priests and laity throughout the world. Following is part of the text of that letter:

". . . And even as Our predecessor of immortal memory, Leo XIII, at the dawn of the twentieth century saw fit to consecrate the whole human race to the Most Sacred Heart of Jesus, so We have likewise in the guise of representative of the whole human family, which He redeemed, the desire to dedicate it in turn to the Immaculate Heart of the Virgin Mary.

"It is Our wish, consequently, that whenever the opportunity suggests itself, this consecration be made in the various dioceses as well as in each of the parishes and families. And We are confident that abundant blessings and favors from Heaven will surge forth from this private and public consecration . . ."

(Signed Pope Pius XII)

On July 7, 1952, Pope Pius XII consecrated the world, and particularly the Russian people, to the Immaculate Heart of Mary. Pope Paul VI consecrated the world to Our Lady's Immaculate Heart in 1964. And on May 13, 1982 Pope John Paul II, uniting himself in intention with the world's bishops, consecrated the world, with a particular mention of Russia, to the Immaculate Heart of Mary. ("In a particular way we entrust and consecrate to thee those individuals and nations which particularly need to be entrusted and consecrated.")

Yet even this singular act did not exactly fulfill the specific request of Our Lady for a Collegial Consecration of Russia by the Holy Father *"in union with all the bishops of the world."* According to Sister Lucia, God will permit the grace of the Collegial Consecration only "when a sufficient number are complying with the message of Fatima."

Thus, the prayers and penances of the faithful are still urgently needed in order to win this grace from Heaven. A most efficacious way to beseech Our Lady for this grace is by consecration of individual dioceses, parishes, and families, as well as of ourselves individually, in response to the call of Pope Pius XII.

Part III
FATIMA, THE UNITED STATES AND THE FUTURE

Not much was heard about Fatima in the United States until World War II began, and particularly until the consecration by the Holy Father in 1942. Since that time, a steady stream of new literature has been made available on the subject. Many excellent books have been written, pamphlets printed in the millions, lectures and sermons delivered, articles published in many magazines and newspapers, plays and radio dramas enacted—all about the remarkable apparitions of Our Lady at Fatima.

However, in spite of all this, it is evident that out of all the millions who hear, only a few take the message to heart and put it into practice in their daily lives. Each passing day brings additional proof, with a more complete fulfillment of the dire predictions made by Our Lady at Fatima in 1917. Already we have fought World War II; less than 5 years later American soldiers were dying in Korea; and a decade after that we were involved in Vietnam; nations have been destroyed; there has been much famine and bitter persecution; and

Communists now rule some 1.8 billion people (about 60% of the world's population)—*all because men refuse to amend their lives and give up sin.*

This is particularly true in our country, where men hear for a while, and then return to their former evil ways, as a frank look at life in the United States will reveal.

LIFE IN THE UNITED STATES

While those on the side of Almighty God and His Blessed Mother try to spread her "peace plan from Heaven," the forces of evil are meeting with even greater success in their efforts to draw men into sin— and Our Lady said at Fatima that *"Wars are a punishment from God for sin."*

Everywhere in this country there has been a tremendous increase in abortions, divorce, birth control, immorality, paganism, materialism and secularism. Pope Pius XII once said: *"The greatest sin of our generation is that it has lost all sense of sin."*

How true these words are becomes apparent when the statements of Jacinta concerning immorality are recalled, and we see that in the United States:

1. At least 1.5 million surgical abortions are performed every year in the United States—one out of every four pregnancies. (Abortion is murder, and murder is one of the "Four Sins Crying to Heaven for Vengeance.") Thus in one year, twice as many Americans are killed through abortion as in all the

wars of U.S. history. Every 11 days more children are aborted than American men were killed in the 11-year-long Vietnam War; every 10 weeks the number totals the number of American war dead in World War II. Every five hours and 15 minutes there are 900 abortions in the United States; each year abortion kills as many as the combined populations of Kansas City, Minneapolis and Miami. Surgical abortion is the most common operation performed in the United States today, three times as common as tonsillectomies. In addition, there are millions of silent abortions caused by the most commonly used (low dosage) birth control pill, the IUD, the morning-after pill, "menstrual extraction" and self-aborting vaginal suppositories. In America the pregnancy rate is high, but the birthrate is very low.

2. One out of every two marriages ends in divorce—50%!—with resultant broken homes, misery for children, etc.

3. Advocates of birth control—insisting that children are a burden and not a blessing—are successfully inducing millions of young couples to use contraceptives. They say in effect that God can create life but cannot provide for it. It is estimated that 1/3 of couples married 10 years or more have been voluntarily sterilized.

4. Homosexuality is being recognized more and more as a "legitimate lifestyle," even by many who call themselves Catholic. (And homosexuality, according to the Bible, is also one of the "Four Sins Crying to Heaven for Vengeance.") San Francisco, one of

our greatest cities, is now considered by many as the capital of homosexuality in the U.S.; "gay" organizations operate openly there and often brazenly stage public rallies in the city streets.

5. Prostitution, juvenile delinquency, sex crimes, and immorality in general have increased to an alarming degree since World War II. Much of this has been caused by the indecent fashions worn by modern women today, and much by the filthy propaganda reaching Americans through the movies, television, radio, newspapers, and particularly through the overwhelming torrent of indecent literature which has deluged us the past several years.

6. Money, material possessions, fame and power have become the "gods" worshipped by millions of Americans today—a man's success in life is now measured by what he has. It little matters how he gets what he has.

7. Too many men and women (and even children) are now turning to drink and drugs—instead of to God—for the solution to life's problems. As a result, they create an even greater problem for themselves, their families, and all with whom they come into contact.

8. Worst of all, there is an organized attempt, which is coming out into the open more all the time, to deny the existence of God, and to destroy Him in the minds of the youth of our country. The coins of our nation proclaim: *"In God we Trust"*—yet, in 1948 the Supreme Court through the McCollum case rul-

ing banned any teaching of religion in our public schools. And several years later the Supreme Court outlawed prayer in public school classrooms.

All of these and many other crimes will combine to bring down upon us the wrath of God in the form of suffering, persecution and even atomic war—that may well be the end of our civilization.

WHAT OF THE FUTURE?

It is sin that is destroying the world today. Since not enough people are willing to grant the requests of Our Lady at Fatima and give up sin, what does the future hold in store for us?

A few months after the close of World War II—the bloodiest in all history—Our Holy Father warned: *"Men must prepare themselves for suffering such as mankind has never seen."*

The Vicar of Christ indicates that we must prepare for suffering even worse than the deluge, which wiped out the whole human race except for Noah and his family—for suffering worse than all the wars and disasters that have been the long history of mankind!

Yes, this is what the future holds for America and the world—suffering such as mankind has never seen— unless a sufficient number of people still can be found willing to grant the requests of Our Lady of Fatima!

IS THERE ANY HOPE?

No matter how late the hour, so long as these threatened disasters have not yet struck, there is still hope of averting them if enough people will amend their lives and do what God asks. We read in the Old Testament *(Jonas* 3) that Almighty God sent Jonas the prophet to warn the people of Nineveh that in 40 days their city would be destroyed. Upon receiving the news, the king immediately proclaimed fasting and abstinence, told the people to don sackcloth and ashes, to do great penance and give up the evil and iniquity in their hearts—and they did. Almighty God was pleased, and at the end of 40 days Nineveh was still standing. God had spared the city because enough reparation had been made.

We also read in the Old Testament *(Genesis* 18) that God would have spared the wicked cities of Sodom and Gomorrah had there been found only 10 just people in them.

Today, Almighty God will spare the world, or at least the United States, from the horrible punishment predicted for us if, proportionately, the "10 just men" can be found willing to make reparation—willing to follow Our Lady of Fatima's "peace plan from Heaven."

Part IV
PUTTING THE PEACE PLAN
INTO ACTION

History has recorded as already having taken place many of the terrible disasters predicted by the Mother of God in 1917. These things cannot be undone. But we still have the future ahead of us. It can be a happy future, filled with peace, if we live our lives according to Our Lady's requests.

These requests, 1) penance and reparation, 2) the daily recitation of the Rosary, 3) the five First Saturdays, and 4) consecration to the Immaculate Heart of Mary, form the "peace plan from Heaven"— our only hope.

PENANCE AND REPARATION

By penance, Our Lady explained that men must amend their lives, give up their easy lives of sin, ask pardon for their sins, and make reparation to the Sacred Heart of Jesus and the Immaculate Heart of Mary, so grievously offended by the sins of men.

By reparation, Our Lady means 1) offering sacrifice to atone for our sins, 2) fulfilling our daily duties to the best of our abilities, 3) accepting the responsibilities of our state in life, 4) obeying the Commandments of God.

The sacrifice Our Lord requires of each of us is that sacrifice necessary to avoid sin and the occasion of sin and to accept with submission all the suffering sent to us. Also, we should make everything we do a sacrifice, and in offering it to God, we should say this prayer: *"O my Jesus, I offer this for love of Thee, for the conversion of poor sinners, and in reparation for all the sins committed against the Immaculate Heart of Mary."*

THE DAILY ROSARY

Our Lady pleaded and insisted that men must say the daily Rosary. Reparation holds back the hand of God from striking the world in just punishment for its many crimes. The Rosary is like a sword or weapon the Mother of God can use to cut down heresy and the forces of evil. It is most powerful, and many times it has saved the world from situations as bad as, if not worse than, the one facing us today.

Four centuries ago, the Turks were overrunning all Europe, and seemed on the verge of wiping out Christianity. When all seemed lost, Pope St. Pius V organized a great Rosary Crusade. The Christian soldiers literally went into battle with swords in one hand and rosaries in the other. On October 7, 1571, at Lepanto, one of the greatest military upsets in all history took place. The smaller Christian fleet, greatly outnumbered, defeated the mighty Turkish Armada, and Christendom was saved—all through the power of the Rosary.

In early 1964, the country of Brazil was within days of falling to Communism. The courageous Archbishop of Rio de Janeiro broadcast radio appeals for prayer and penance in keeping with Our Lady's Fatima requests. The response of Brazilians rose and rose until it culminated in a vast march of 600,000 Rosary-praying women in Sao Paulo on March 19. More such marches were scheduled, but on April 1, the Communists fled the country, and freedom was preserved.

Today, we are threatened on all sides by Communism. But the Blessed Virgin Mary can overcome these forces of evil overnight—if enough people will say the daily Rosary. Pope Pius IX said: *"Give me an army saying the Rosary, and I will conquer the world."*

Particularly is the Family Rosary recommended, for *"the family that prays together stays together,"* and today our families are threatened with breakup on all sides.

After each decade of the Rosary, you should recite the prayer: *"O my Jesus, forgive us our sins, save us from the fire of Hell, lead all souls to Heaven, especially those who have most need of Thy mercy."*

THE FIVE FIRST SATURDAYS

This devotion consists in 1) going to Confession, 2) receiving Holy Communion, 3) reciting 5 decades of the Rosary, and 4) spending 15 minutes with Our Lady meditating on the mysteries of the Rosary—all with the intention of making reparation to her.

The Mediatrix of All Graces has promised, at the hour of death, all graces necessary for salvation to those who faithfully practice this devotion for the First Saturday of any five consecutive months. (NOTE: *The Confession may be made under the usual condition of 8 days before or after Holy Communion, provided the person is not in the state of mortal sin when he receives Holy Communion.)*

The first Friday, first Saturday, and first Sunday of the month normally come together in the same week. The Confession good for one is good for the others. It is recommended that people receive Holy Communion in reparation on all three days, giving Our Lady a little more than she asks—and helping to make up for those who refuse to give her anything at all.

In addition to assisting at the Holy Sacrifice of the Mass, receiving Holy Communion is the most perfect form of reparation that can be offered.

CONSECRATION TO THE IMMACULATE HEART OF MARY

This consecration is the least understood but one of the most important parts of the message of Fatima. Our Lady is looking for people willing to become cells of prayer and sacrifice through consecration to her.

Personal consecration to the Immaculate Heart of Mary can take many forms. It can be done simply by reciting *with sincerity* the act of consecration printed further on. This consecration can be renewed each day merely by saying the morning offering to the Sacred Heart of Jesus. However, the act itself should be repeated on all important feast days of the Blessed Mother. *More important than reciting the act is to live up to the conditions which it sets forth, particularly by fulfilling Our Lady's requests at Fatima.* In consecrating oneself to Mary, a Christian pays her homage,

24

places himself in her service and under her protection, and strives to imitate her virtues.

One of the best forms of consecration for the average layman is to wear the Brown Scapular of Our Lady of Mount Carmel. Sister Lucia has said that all Catholics should wear the Brown Scapular as part of the Fatima message. She said, *"The Rosary and the Scapular are inseparable."* The Brown Scapular of Mt. Carmel is an abbreviated form of the large Scapular worn by members of the Carmelite Order; thus it can be called a "holy habit" and "Our Lady's livery." A person who wears this Scapular declares that he or she belongs to Mary. In return, the Mother of God has promised eternal life to those who die wearing this mantle. In 1251, when she gave the Scapular to St. Simon Stock and thereby to the world, the Queen of Heaven stated: *"Whosoever dies clothed in this shall never suffer eternal fire."* Wearing the Scapular serves as a constant reminder of one's personal consecration to Mary and of the necessity of imitating her virtues and heeding her requests.

NOTE: The Scapular Medal may be substituted when it is impossible or impractical to wear the cloth Scapular. However, to be worn validly, the person wearing the medal must first have been enrolled in the cloth Scapular, and the medal must be blessed by a priest. It is not necessary to have the cloth Scapulars blessed.

TRUE DEVOTION, ONE OF THE MOST PERFECT FORMS OF CONSECRATION

Another excellent but more difficult form of consecration is the practice of True Devotion to the Blessed

Virgin Mary, as preached by St. Louis Grignion De Montfort. This consists in giving oneself as a servant or a "slave" to the Blessed Mother, so one can be used as an instrument of God's mercy in drawing the souls of poor sinners to the Sacred Heart of Jesus through the Immaculate Heart of Mary. This means giving to Mary all our thoughts, words, actions, sufferings and possessions, plus, the merits from our good works, that she may use them as she sees fit in reparation for sin, for the conversion of poor sinners, and for the greater love and honor and glory of God.

St. Louis De Montfort says that as Christ came to us through Mary, He desires that we come to Him through her. The Saint states that by consecrating ourselves to the Immaculate Heart of Mary we consecrate ourselves to the Sacred Heart of Jesus, for the two are one. All we do for Mary, we do for Jesus; all we ask of her, we ask of Him; and Our Lord cannot refuse if His Blessed Mother intercedes for us.

Since she desires and requests it, can we choose a more perfect form of consecration to Jesus than through the Immaculate Heart of His Holy Mother?

HER IMMACULATE HEART
WILL TRIUMPH

At Fatima, Our Lady promised that in the end her Immaculate Heart will triumph, Russia will be converted, and some time of peace will be granted to the world.

That final triumph can come soon, without a lot of

blood being shed, if enough people will still grant the requests she made at Fatima. Or, it can come after an atomic war, or more terrible disasters, that may see the greater part of humanity wiped off the face of the earth.

It depends upon how many of us are willing to follow Our Lady's "peace plan from Heaven."

"WHAT CAN I DO?"

1. Start by observing Our Lady's requests at Fatima:
   a. Consecrate yourself to the Immaculate Heart of Mary.
   b. Offer up your daily tasks as a sacrifice in reparation for your own sins and the sins of others.
   c. Say the Rosary every day.
   d. Wear the Brown Scapular as a sign of personal consecration to Mary, and make acts of reparation to her Immaculate Heart.
   e. Make the 5 First Saturdays with the attendant 15 minutes of meditation on the Mysteries of the Rosary in company with Mary.
   f. Make visits to the Blessed Sacrament in reparation for sins against her Immaculate Heart.
   g. Do extra penances and say extra prayers for the conversion of sinners.

2. Begin today to reform your life completely and to orient it toward God. Determine, with God's grace, to become a saint. Engage in spiritual reading every day.

3. Distribute extra copies of this booklet. It is a brief but complete statement on Fatima.

4. Ask Our Lady to guide you in your vocation and to give you an apostolate suitable to your station in life.

5. Say the prayers taught by Our Lady and the Angel at Fatima.

HOW TO SAY THE ROSARY

The whole Rosary is composed of fifteen decades. Each decade is recited in honor of a mystery of Our Lord's life and that of His Blessed Mother, beginning with the *Annunciation* to Mary of the Incarnation and ending with Mary's triumphal *Coronation* in Heaven. A decade consists of one *Our Father,* ten *Hail Marys* and a *Glory be to the Father.* The ordinary beads or chaplet contain five decades, since it is customary to recite five decades at a time while meditating on one set of mysteries.

FORM:

Sign of the Cross
The *Apostles' Creed* on the crucifix
The *Our Father* on the large beads
The *Hail Mary* on the small beads
Glory be to the Father, after the last *Hail Mary* of each
    decade

Before reciting each decade, name a mystery of the Rosary (in sequence) and meditate on it during the decade.

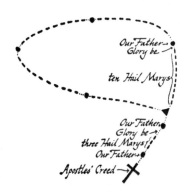

THE FIFTEEN DECADES OF THE ROSARY

THE JOYFUL MYSTERIES

To be said on all Mondays and Thursdays and all Sundays of Advent.

1. *The Annunciation*—Mary learns from the Angel Gabriel that God wishes her to be the mother of God, and she humbly accepts. *(Luke 1:26–38)*
2. *The Visitation*—Mary goes to visit her cousin Elizabeth and is hailed by her as "blessed among women." *(Luke 1:39–56)*
3. *The Nativity*—Mary gives birth to Jesus in the stable at Bethlehem. *(Luke 2:1–20)*
4. *The Presentation*—Mary and Joseph present Jesus to His Heavenly Father in the Temple of Jerusalem forty days after His birth. *(Luke 2:22–39)*
5. *The Finding In The Temple*—After searching for three days, Mary and Joseph find the twelve-year-old Jesus sitting in the Temple with the learned doctors. *(Luke 2:42–52)*

To be said on all Tuesdays and Fridays and all Sundays of Lent.

1. *The Agony In The Garden*—The thought of our sins and of His coming sufferings causes the agonizing Saviour to sweat blood. *(Luke 22:41–45)*
2. *The Scourging*—Jesus is stripped and unmercifully scourged until His body is one mass of bloody wounds. *(Matt. 27:26)*
3. *The Crowning With Thorns*—Jesus' claim to Kingship is ridiculed by a crown of thorns being placed on His head and a reed in His hand. *(Matt. 27:28–31)*
4. *The Carrying Of The Cross*—Jesus shoulders His own cross and carries it to the place of crucifixion, while Mary follows Him sorrowing. *(Luke 23:26–32)*
5. *The Crucifixion*—Jesus dies, nailed to the cross, after three hours of agony witnessed by His Mother. *(Matt. 27:33–50)*

THE GLORIOUS MYSTERIES

To be said on all Sundays (except Advent and Lent) and all Wednesdays and Saturdays.

1. *The Resurrection*—Jesus rises from the dead on Easter Sunday, glorious and immortal, as He had predicted. *(Matt. 28:5)*
2. *The Ascension*—Jesus ascends into Heaven forty days after His Resurrection to sit at the right hand of God the Father from whence He shall return to judge the living and the dead at the end of the world. *(Luke 24:50–51)*

3. *The Descent Of The Holy Spirit*—Jesus sends the Holy Spirit in the form of fiery tongues upon His Apostles and disciples. *(Acts 2:2–4)*

4. *The Assumption*—Mary's soul returns to God and her glorified body is assumed into Heaven and reunited with her soul.

5. *The Coronation*—Mary is crowned as Queen of Heaven and Earth, Queen of Angels and Saints, that she may rule over all hearts in time and in eternity.

ACT OF CONSECRATION
TO THE IMMACULATE HEART OF MARY

O MARY, VIRGIN most powerful and Mother of Mercy, Queen of Heaven and Refuge of Sinners, we consecrate ourselves to thy Immaculate Heart. We consecrate to thee our very being and our whole life: all that we have, all that we love, all that we are. To thee we give our bodies, our hearts, and our souls; to thee we give our homes, our families and our country. We desire that all that is in us and around us may belong to thee and may share in the benefits of thy motherly blessing. And, that this act of consecration may be truly fruitful and lasting, we renew this day at thy feet the promises of our Baptism and our First Holy Communion. We pledge ourselves to profess courageously and at all times the truths of our holy Faith, and to live as befits Catholics, who are submissive to all directions of the Pope and the bishops in communion with him. We pledge ourselves to keep the Commandments of God and of His Church, in particular to keep holy the Lord's Day. We pledge ourselves to make the consoling practices of the Christian religion, and above all, Holy Communion, an important part of our lives, in so far as we shall be able to do.

Finally, we promise thee, O glorious Mother of God and loving Mother of men, to devote ourselves wholeheartedly to the spreading of devotion to thy Immaculate Heart, in order to hasten and assure, through the queenly rule of thy Immaculate Heart, the coming of the kingdom of the Sacred Heart of thy adorable Son, in our own hearts and in those of all men, in our country, and in all the world, as in Heaven, so on earth. Amen.

THE FATIMA PRAYERS

"O my God, I believe, I adore, I hope and I love Thee. I ask pardon for those who do not believe, do not adore, do not hope and do not love Thee."

"Most Holy Trinity—Father, Son, and Holy Spirit—I adore Thee profoundly. I offer Thee the most precious Body, Blood, Soul and Divinity of Jesus Christ, present in all the tabernacles of the world, in reparation for the outrages, sacrileges and indifferences whereby He is offended. And through the infinite merits of His Most Sacred Heart and the Immaculate Heart of Mary, I beg of Thee the conversion of poor sinners."

"O my Jesus, I offer this for love of Thee, for the conversion of sinners, and in reparation for the sins committed against the Immaculate Heart of Mary." (To be said when offering up personal sacrifices, penances, sufferings, etc.)

"O my Jesus, forgive us our sins, save us from the fire of Hell, lead all souls to Heaven, especially those who have most need of Thy mercy." (To be said after the *Glory Be to the Father* following each decade of the Rosary.)